ILLUMINATIAM

THE FIRST TESTAMENT
OF THE
ILLUMINATI

ILLUMINATIAM

THE FIRST TESTAMENT

OF THE

ILLUMINATI

CONTENTS

The production of this publication
has been authorized by the Illuminati. Its
authenticity has been confirmed by the
Department of Verifications.

To verify the authenticity of this
document and its contents, visit

ILLUMINATI.AM/VERIFIED

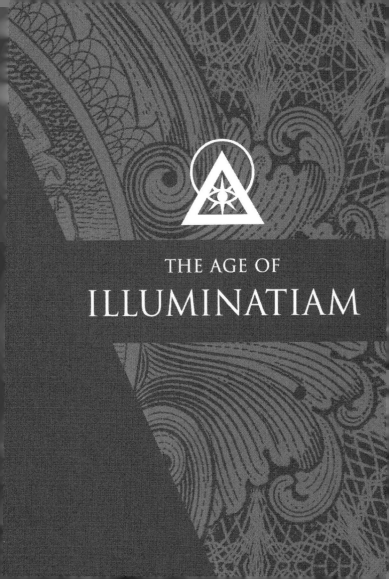

THE AGE OF
ILLUMINATIAM

1

W ELCOME. THE ILLUMINATI holds you, a citizen of our shared planet, in the highest esteem.

You may not realize it yet but you have been led here by design, even though you arrived by your own free will.

You were not shown a symbol in the sky nor did you hear a magnified voice that caused the ground beneath you to tremble, demanding you read the words written in this testament. You followed your own life's journey to find your way here — never suspecting that the map you relied upon was drawn by us.

The Illuminati is an elite collective of political leaders, business owners, and other influential members of this planet. Our organization unites leaders of the world in an unrestrictive and private domain — free of political, religious, and geographical boundaries — to further the prosperity of the human species. To operate in humanity's best interest, our council's authority supersedes that of individual governments, making decisions that your queens, presidents, emperors, and other leaders may be unable to decree on their own, but are required to carry out.

You will not find us praised in any history book or document, though the Illuminati has helped shape every major movement on this planet since the first human government was established.

THE ILLUMINATI'S PURPOSE IS TO SECURE THE ONGOING SURVIVAL OF THE HUMAN SPECIES.

Like all organisms, the human species naturally strives against extinction. Though your countries have borders and your languages have barriers, all people in all places are members of the same biological family. All humans are pieces of a collective that keeps humanity in existence.

Though you are merely a speck on the back of a grain of sand when compared to the vast number of humans born and decomposed for millennia, you are as important to your species' survival as the greatest kings and queens. If every human of Earth was suddenly exterminated at once, sparing only two beggars, they would each be owners of half a planet, and the only hopes left for humanity's future.

If only all humans understood their importance in the grand scale of survival. If only all humans could see that barriers between belief or geography or skin are of no importance to the perpetuation of their species. If only all humans saw themselves as tiny but uniquely important pieces of our Universal Design.

But by nature, the human is affected by instinct, emotion, and imbalance. A human will turn on one of its own species for reasons that will never matter in a thousand years, and likely not matter in even a hundred or ten. While you have seen the Light in the distance and chosen to follow it — even if from mere curiosity — there are millions more whose backs are turned against its glow.

FREEDOM IS AN IDOL OF THE HUMAN SPECIES.

The Illuminati operates in defense of you and all humans, in all places, and of all generations. Our duty to this planet has spanned across centuries and survived even the most established government entities. But the cultivation of trillions of human lives is a daunting responsibility, and while the human would not exist today without our protection, many uninformed masses mistake our guidance for a restriction of liberty.

Every human desires to be free of oppression, free of hardship, free of poverty, free of hunger, free of rules and laws — but as you understand, the nature of your species leaves true freedom impossible.

Are you free to murder? Are you free to steal? Are others free to murder and steal from you? Or are there certain freedoms that must be given up for the benefit of all?

FOR HAPPINESS, THE HUMAN DESIRES FREEDOM; FOR PROSPERITY, THE HUMAN REQUIRES LEADERSHIP.

This is the reason behind our anonymity. To continue functioning throughout societal changes and generational differences, the Illuminati must remain behind the curtain — an outsider, belonging to none and loyal to all.

You may never understand how your life can be free while guided by our organization. You may never fully comprehend our purpose and why you are safest and happiest with us. Simply open your mind and release your apprehensions, and you will find the relief of truth.

We will never take your hand and pull you down the path like a slave to our whims. You must find and travel the road on your own. But your quality of life is our greatest concern and the reason we leave a map for you to follow if you desire.

OUR SYMBOLS PERMEATE HUMAN SOCIETY AS SUBTLE DIRECTIONS TO THE TRUTH.

Many of your brethren have noticed our symbology in artwork, architecture, and visual media. Such displays of loyalty are highly appreciated. However our symbols are not placed in your world for our own glorification, but instead serve as gentle instructions for those who look up from the rocks of Earth and choose to follow the Light.

Perhaps it was one of these directions that brought you here, or maybe a hundred of them scattered throughout your streets and buildings and glowing screens since your childhood. An invisible chain reaction of events in your life, paired with similar events in the lives of those around you, have all fallen in perfect place, like the toppling of countless lines of dominoes that meet in the center. While you pushed the dominos, it was us who laid them in a line.

YOUR LIFE'S JOURNEY HAS LED YOU TO THIS MOMENT.

Hope is in the distance. The age of War is coming to an end. Terrors that have plagued humanity for millennia will soon be obsolete and forgotten. Every year is a thread in a rich and glorious tapestry that is approaching its completion. Your ancestors lived through the darkness of night, but your descendants will live in the Abundance of the new dawn.

This book is your guide: the first testament of the coming age of Illuminatiam. It is order amidst a world of chaos, a candle for all who travel the path as the night reaches its darkest point. It is a promise that even as you bear every hardship that slams against you like gusts of wind fighting to turn you around, each step forward brings you closer to the joy of Abundance.

We invite you to discover more about our organization and to understand your role in this planetary union. Answers to many of your questions are contained in these pages: our methods, our developing technologies, the sources of our wealth, the future of your world, and the root of our power.

In creating this book, we hope to alleviate the concerns voiced by your people and provide insight into our plan for the human species. While our daily operations must remain confidential for your safety, we strive to create a better understanding between us and those we have been entrusted to protect.

THIS BOOK CONTAINS TRUTHS ABOUT YOUR WORLD.

Before you read any further, you must understand with greatest severity that everything inside this book is either true or cannot be safely divulged at this time. Choosing whether or not to believe is your freedom.

Some might ask: why would a global organization relinquish their hold upon their deepest secrets in such a public manner? Why risk turning a population against us when secrecy has served so well?

Because our enemies will do nothing.

The things you will read have been in effect for decades, but they were already being planned decades earlier than that. Anyone who reads this book as a means to subvert our authority will find their scheme to be futile. The components are so deeply established in your society, there is nothing anyone could do to change them even if they

tried. Not even the world's most powerful leaders can alter planetary law.

APPROACH THIS BOOK WITH A MIND THAT IS OPEN FOR REVELATION.

To truly comprehend what you are
about to read, you must empty yourself
of all preconceived ideas, clear your
subconscious of every notion you might
have about the world around you, and
prepare to accept new ideas you might
never have considered to be true.

However, most who read this book will not. Most will dismiss it. Few will finish it, and many of those who do will discard it immediately after.

In fact, we are so certain of our influence over your mind — and the media we have bombarded it with since before your conception — that we haven't the slightest fear of you doing something about anything you read within its pages.

There will always be a voice that tells you this is not real, no matter how quietly it may whisper. Our hold upon your subconscious will incline you to dismiss this as a hoax, something you needn't worry about for more than humor. Something you needn't investigate further. Something you can simply do nothing about, and can abandon by the wayside of a path half-journeyed.

But even if you are skeptical, there will always be a part of you that will wonder if it is all true. There will always be a voice that whispers in your ear, "press onward, the Light is just ahead."

Once your eyes are opened, you can never go back to the childlike safety of ignorance. Read on only if you accept this burden, but fear not for what is ahead. You are never alone.

WE ARE ALWAYS WATCHING OUT FOR YOU.

THE

MARK

THE
PYRAMID

Life's journey begins at the bottom, where many reside but few rise above. All levels are important: without a foundation, the structure could not exist. As a person climbs the great Pyramid, it becomes clear that they have always been one part of our universe's most intricate mechanism.

THE
LIGHT

The world is covered in a darkness of confusion, war, and hardship. The Light is an ever-present guidance: an unseen and unnamed higher power that compels those who follow it to strive for the betterment of the human species, and rewards those who do. All who seek its glow act as mirrors, reflecting the Light into the world's still-darkened spaces.

THE
EYE

The Eye resides at the center of the Light, its focus so fixed upon truth that it becomes a beacon for the glow. Those who follow the Light are central to this planet's Universal Design. Ever watchful and ever vigilant, the Eye sees and knows all just as a shepherd sees and knows all of the flock.

THE
ETERNAL

The Illuminati's duty to this planet
has spanned across centuries and
survived even the most established
government entities. Though not
praised in any history book, we have
shaped every major movement on
this planet and guided the human
species through every threat of
extinction. Though our human
members may perish and fade into
the annals of time, the Illuminati
will continue to stand into eternity.

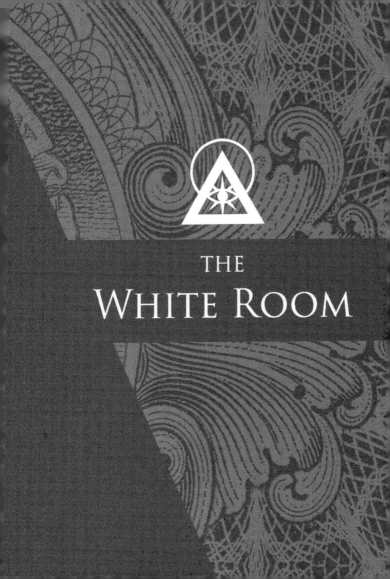

THE
WHITE ROOM

2

I N THE ATLANTIC OCEAN IS AN
island that does not appear
on any map, and never will.
It has no official name. Those who
have visited call it The Isle.

Protected in the embrace of an
ocean, then sand, then five miles of trees
and camouflaged razor wire, is a building

made of concrete and steel. If you flew over it, you'd see it as a flat gray plateau dotted by misted square skylights. Their glass is so thick, a missile could ram into its center, detonate, and only leave its own bits and guts littered against the ground.

Two planes have crashed directly into it but left no mark besides the faint black ash that still coats the taller tree trunks. Both planes ventured off their course and found themselves lost in the airspace of The Isle, and after spotting the strip of open space between the trees, attempted to make emergency landings. This proved impossible: the plane in 1998 was tangled by razor wire on its descent, and the plane in 2014 malfunctioned as it entered the magnetized security zone and its electrical systems overloaded.

Neither casualties were intentional. The Isle has no human operators and runs as its own machine. Through two vault doors protected by password and retinal authentication, there is an elevator that descends deep into the ground and opens to the White Room. The future of your planet is decided here.

THE MOST TERRIFYING FEAR OF SOMEONE WITH POWER IS LOSING THE POWER THAT MAKES THEM SOMEONE.

Your leaders — regardless of your opinion of their character or ability — have all surpassed every imaginable threat to become who they are today, whether by merit or conspiracy. But the humans they govern are easily swayed by emotion and instinct, and your leaders will not risk their life's work on the whims of manipulatable minds.

For this reason, we meet in the White Room.

Its ceilings are eight feet high and the walls are made of crisp, smooth white stone without any decoration. The room is shaped in a perfect rectangle with only the elevator as both entrance and exit. Once the door seals, there are no lights inside nor electricity to power them. It is a smothering darkness experienced only in the deepest of caves, and if not for candles, it would drive the sanest person into fits of madness within days.

In the center of the room sits a table and chairs made entirely of transparent glass. From anywhere in the room, you can see everything that is happening. The transparent table ensures that no recording devices are hidden in the hands and that secret notes are not written. The nondescript walls of stone deep beneath the ground protect against devices embedded in the body or any communication with the outside world.

Even the participants, regardless of if they are presidents or queens or owners of multinational corporations, immediately strip of all belongings and leave their clothing in the elevator. They don robes as white as the room that surrounds them and carry only a thick candle through the doors — its wax is scanned before entry.

Despite all of these precautions, every person who enters is required to investigate the room from top to bottom. Trust does not exist in this place, even amongst friends and allies. None are offended: being wary is honesty. All in power are ruthless and know better than to trust others like themselves.

They come to the White Room not for secrecy, but for the truest of freedom. Things discussed in the White Room will never be revealed, seen, nor heard by anyone who is not present. Anything can be said or done in the room without fear of repercussions, retaliation, or risk to a leader's claim to power. Decisions can be made for the betterment of the human species without any worry of persecution from the very humans they gather to protect.

THERE IS NO FREEDOM FOR THOSE WHO PROTECT THE FREEDOMS OF THEIR BROTHERS AND SISTERS.

If what is said and decided inside the White Room was to ever reach the ears of anyone outside, the entire structure of this planet would be upended by civil war. The human species is easily swayed: it thinks reasonably when at ease but acts erratically when under pressure.

Humans react before understanding the complete repercussions of their deeds, following instinct with little regard to what their actions might affect in ten or a hundred or a thousand years.

Thriving empires have fallen at the hands of its own people. By the time they see what they have done, it is already too late to go back.

The Illuminati is free of this restraint. Decisions made in the White Room are not bound by belief or allegiance or generation, but are on behalf of all humans on the planet now and in the future. These decisions are made to ensure the survival of all as a collective, no matter how unpopular they might be if put to a public vote.

There are no political parties or prejudices in the White Room. Outside its walls, those present may fight wars against each other that end the lives of scores of their kin; but inside the room they are all cogs in a Universal Design that is bigger than their petty, temporary differences.

There is no animosity inside: all are equal, and all have a duty to fulfill.

Everything decided within the walls of the White Room is for you.

You may think that a room of people you do not know, and who are humans like yourself, should not make decisions regarding your life. Are you merely a pawn in a game being played by others? Shouldn't you control your own life?

Do not allow yourself to be convinced that freedom is what you desire because this is how you and those who live around you are controlled. You are told that you have freedom while freedom is defined by those with power.

TRUE POWER BEGINS WITH THE RELINQUISHING OF CONTROL.

True power grows from the comprehension that while one's place in the universe can be microscopically small, it is still immensely important. True power thrives on the understanding that while freedom is naturally desired by humans, it is merely a placebo to alleviate feelings of chaos — a chaos that can only be harnessed by order.

A skyscraper may tower over a city but it is only as tall as the molecules in its materials. The Illuminati may thrive but we are only as strong as the people we protect. We were born as one of you; we will die as one of you.

The safeguards of the White Room are not devised to keep you out. You know you are different from most others who surround you, though civility requires you to keep such thoughts to yourself. But there are many others whose decisions are still under the reign of their animal instincts. Their lack of understanding would cause them to rise up and wage war against all that keeps their species intact, wrecking the Universal Design that has allowed the human to rise above its animal counterparts.

The safeguards of the White Room are for your protection and the sanctity of the decisions made inside. Many seats remain empty at the table, awaiting those who are willing and able to claim them. If you strive for greatness, and seek out the Light that glows steadily brighter in the distance, you too will be invited to enter its hallowed, white hall.

7137

what is
Illuminios?

Illuminios is the annual conference for ranking members of the Illuminati, held in locations across the planet since 1939. The weekend event consists of addresses from the Illuminati council, the election and initiation of new ranking members, reports from each of the Illuminati's departments, and the dispensation of the following year's directives to all members.

During the weekend, subcommittees meet to discuss objectives for the human species as a whole and weigh specific risks that threaten its existence. Judgement panels also meet to review reported wrongdoings by Illuminati members, and to ascertain if discipline is required.

Heads of the Illuminati's departments are required to attend each year they serve in their position. Other ranking Illuminati members are not required to attend Illuminios and can request transcripts from their liaison.

While the event is unavailable to public citizens, recent policy changes have allowed portions of Illuminios to be rebroadcast via our official online profiles.

Find out more at illuminati.am/illuminios

METHODS OF
MIND CONTROL

3

YOUR MIND IS BEING CON-
trolled at this moment
but you have been
trained to ignore it.

There is no reason to fear. For society to
function in peaceful order, its people
must be guided — even if their
incomprehension would incline them to

deny the very guidance that ensures their safety and survival.

Mind control is an inaccurate term. The mind cannot be truly controlled due to the free will of the subconscious that gives the power of choice to every human. However, though free and independent to make its own decisions, your mind has been trained to respond to subconscious cues that are hidden in the world around you. These act as subtle arrows pointing you in the right direction, while allowing you to choose the road you will take to get there.

THOUGH YOU CHOSE
TO READ THIS BOOK,
IT WAS OUR
SUBCONSCIOUS CUES
THAT LED YOU TO
THIS PAGE.

The influencing of an independent mind requires the decades-long implementation of a societal framework that is built upon the delivery of messages. Only the Illuminati has the resources to build this structure, though many governments have tried to mimic it.

A hundred billion mental triggers bombard your subconscious since the moment you are conceived. A mishmash of signals and waves have been hand-fed to your mind since childhood, seeping inoculations into your brain's synapses through pathways hidden behind colorful screens and microscopic spores.

Our messages have reached your mind since before you were born, carried by every sound your mother listened to as she carried you in her womb. You knew the voice of the Illuminati before we even knew you.

From your first breath, you were trained to respond to our cues. You are inoculated by omnipresent energy waves being broadcast from screens and phones and devices you can never fully avoid.

Many of our delivery systems have been disguised behind things you use in your everyday life. Radio and television waves carry music and video on specific spectrums, broadcasting sounds over the air that cannot be seen nor heard without a device to receive it. In the same way, our messages are broadcast on spectrums only detectible by your subconscious mind, allowing us to gently influence your decisions and choices, and even those of people in entire cities and countries at once.

THE MIND IS THE MOST POWERFUL ELEMENT OF THE HUMAN SPECIES

The mind differentiates the human from all other creatures of this planet. The poor remain poor and the rich remain rich because of what they choose to fill their minds with. This power is invisible and undetectable, but alters more than anything in the physical world.

Our organization remains elusive due to this power. We have altered the mindset of society to ensure a constant disbelief in our existence. Observe how anyone who claims that they have found proof of our influence is quickly alienated by those closest to them. Conspiracy books and movies draw humor out of what is true in order to shroud its accuracies in a mire of comedy. By flooding the planet with false information and leaking incorrect data to those who investigate us, we are able to maintain our anonymity in the mists of confusion.

Even as you read this book, you have been trained to disbelieve it. Even as you are told the greatest truths about your life and the darkest secrets of your species, you may never become entirely convinced that these words are genuine. Even as you study these words for months or years or decades after they have been written, you will be wary. You will scour computer networks for clues of its forgery, you will seek out others who have read its pages to see if they have discovered anything to prove that it is wrong. You will send it to your reporters to verify but receive no accurate response.

There is no sin in doubt. If you choose to read these pages and by its end you still do not believe, there is no need to fear retribution. We cannot hold these feelings in contempt because they were placed in your mind by us on purpose to defend us from prying eyes.

Doubt is the most powerful camouflage the Illuminati uses to remain anonymous. If you do not believe something is real, you will never go looking for it.

does the Illuminati charge a
membership fee?

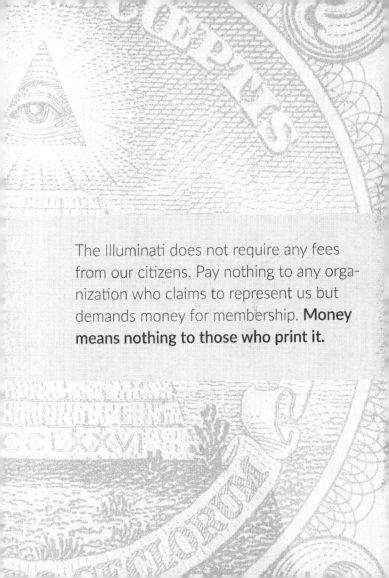

The Illuminati does not require any fees from our citizens. Pay nothing to any organization who claims to represent us but demands money for membership. **Money means nothing to those who print it.**

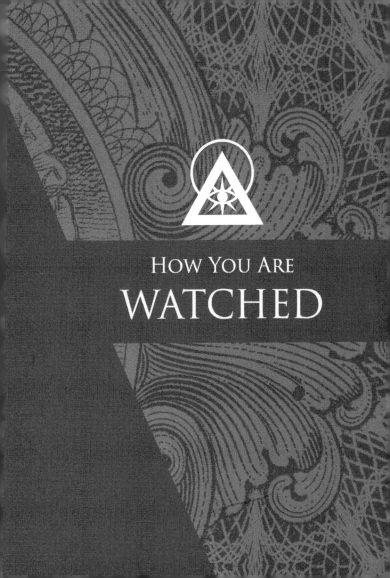

HOW YOU ARE
WATCHED

4

THE INVENTION OF EMAIL IS NO coincidence, nor is the new popularity of text messaging and social media. Their widespread use is the result of a complex operation authorized by the Illuminati to aid in the surveillance of the citizens we govern.

In a private society that lacks technology, communications between potentially dangerous subjects are difficult to monitor. If a pen writes on a piece of paper and the resulting letter is not physically intercepted, a full transmission of information is completed without any indication of its contents.

Plans between anarchists and genocidal murderers cannot be prevented if our associates are not alerted to their creation, leaving citizens open to harm from those who seek depopulation of the planet for their own gain.

In modern times, the leader of a large country strayed from our directives, succumbing to his addiction to power. By siphoning away the resources intended for his people, he was able to stockpile a vast network of wealth. This money was used to finance the construction of biological weapons and the development of a plan to overtake a highly populated country, whose power had made it impenetrable for centuries.

To overtake such an established world power, he schemed a genocide. He planned to propel a rocket into the outer atmosphere of this planet and allow it to fall over the targeted country. Once entering airspace where it might be detected, the rocket would dismantle itself and release a net of large balloons that expanded to reach over a radius of miles. The balloons would contain a viral poison, and when shot down by the defensive agencies of the target, the chemicals would rain upon the people who lived below.

The disease was developed to lose its potency within weeks but had no cure and would spread quickly between hosts. With his naval ships hovering on the coasts to prevent anyone from escaping, every resident of the country would succumb to the effects of the disease and die. Within days, the entire population would be exterminated, leaving a land of bodies to decompose in the sun, and later only dust for his armies to trample upon.

But like all plans by misguided sociopaths, his held a fatally overlooked flaw. While devising his strategy, he communicated via an email system created specifically for messages of high security — forgetting that all electronic messages are actively monitored by our departments. While the conversations he

80

had with his generals in private went unnoticed, his electronic communications could be intercepted due to the fact that they were typed into a computer.

While monitoring private messages may seem invasive, it is for the safety of all humans. Because of the systems we have established, this plan for destruction never reached fruition, and justice was served for his insubordination.

IF THERE IS NO GUILT, THERE IS NO REASON TO HIDE.

The department responsible for monitoring worldwide communications has no need for the private details of the daily lives of our citizens. Our systems remain in place only for your security. There is no risk of any data becoming public knowledge without our authorization.

Humans lie to themselves with a belief in secrecy and security. Corporations devise large-scale methods of anonymity through the use of codes and passwords and aliases, believing that their information is safe from outside eyes — forgetting that the very computers they use were manufactured to broadcast directly to our agencies.

THERE ARE NO SECRETS.

Every computer, phone, or communication tool is a device used to gather information about you. Electronics were proliferated for this very purpose. Billions of terabytes of data are transmitted, reviewed, and stored in secure locations that cannot be destroyed by any threat other than a complete obliteration of this planet.

To truly understand the magnitude of this operation, you must dispel what you have been told and taught throughout your entire life — misdirections we have placed for the security of this initiative. Our surveillance cannot be detected nor deactivated because it exists in the core of every electronic device.

The personal computer's purpose is to gather data on individuals and create profiles of their movements, loyalties, and the level of risk they are to the human species. To ensure the independence of every citizen, we cannot intercept all crimes — unless such actions could affect the human species as a whole.

Our department retains a dossier of every human on earth: every website they have visited, every document they have typed, every image they have scanned, every video they have recorded or broadcast.

WE KNOW AND SEE ALL JUST AS A SHEPHERD KNOWS AND SEES ALL OF HIS FLOCK.

The Illuminati supports various digital initiatives to ensure your safety from global threats. We have propagated safeguards throughout a minimum of 98% of all communication devices currently in operation. The success of our surveillance is the result of public relations campaigns working to

increase societal reliance upon technology.

In 1999, our Illuminios conference
encouraged societal influencers to
increase the public's usage of text
messaging, as these are easier to surveil
than audio phone calls that must be
transcribed.

In 2004, our organization funded the
development of an Internet membership
website to aid in the collection of data
on citizens of interest. Our influencers
were encouraged to use the website and
invite those who follow their lead to do

the same. Our partners created a "tagging" system that recognizes facial features of a person in a photograph or video, no matter which angle they might appear, and launched a campaign to promote its usage.

In this way, our operatives are able to gather a vast amount of information previously unavailable from private citizens. Every photograph and video that is stored on the Internet is immediately tagged by our systems with the identities of every person in the image, regardless of if they are the subject or merely a person in the crowded background. This allows us to track the movements of every single person in a technologically advanced society, even if they themselves do not carry any traceable devices.

A FALSE SENSE OF SECURITY REVEALS THE DEEPEST SECRETS.

Much of our surveillance techniques involve creating systems that claim to be anonymous, therefore attracting those who have things to hide. Online anonymity networks have seen increased usage amongst those who require the utmost privacy. Its users openly reveal their deepest secrets behind onion layers of protection, not realizing that the network they rely upon is of our invention and specifically created to trace their movements.

The technology in use by private citizens is already 20 years behind that of the United States military, and theirs is 50 years behind what has already been developed in our laboratories. With unlimited resources at our disposal, our organization can invest billions into the research and creation of any technology required by our work.

The focus of our future objectives has turned to increasing the popularity of cloud storage services and computing. By encouraging citizens to store files in a remote location that is secure and easy to access, their private documents and information are volunteered eagerly for our surveillance.

Even the mightiest kings will fall because of secrets. We know of everything. We know of the message a politician sent that may seem to be long-gone history but would lead him to suicide if his spouse was to see it. We know of the worst mistakes and the worst sins ever committed by everyone in power.

THE ILLUMINATI IS FORGIVING BUT THE PEOPLE ARE NOT.

When our ranking members stray from our directives and require judgment, their punishment is shame. It is for this reason you often read of celebrities and public figures who suddenly face scandals but remain silent amidst the backlash. As their careers crumble, they know there is nothing they can do — they knew our judgment was approaching weeks before it appeared.

The sanctity of our authority must be upheld amongst every human, even those who believe they are powerful enough to disobey. The Illuminati's purpose is the preservation of the human species and thus we avoid causing death to even our worst perpetrators.

Leaders of the world fear little but death and losing their power. Public shame is a warning shot: one that is rarely ignored. The punished who receive judgment with humility are often restored to their previous glory at the end of their sentence.

Every person is human and every human makes mistakes, but buried in those mistakes are scandals of abject ruin. You will deny that you have secrets when in reality you know exactly the secrets we are referring to.

Your loyalty is your armor and protection. There is no reason to fear any public dissemination of your secrets. It is highly unlikely that any human has even observed your dossier in our database, as they are sorted and filtered by an electronic algorithm to identify risks. Find security in knowing that while your secrets are safe, the secrets of all who strive to destroy your species are also in our hands, and can and will be used against them.

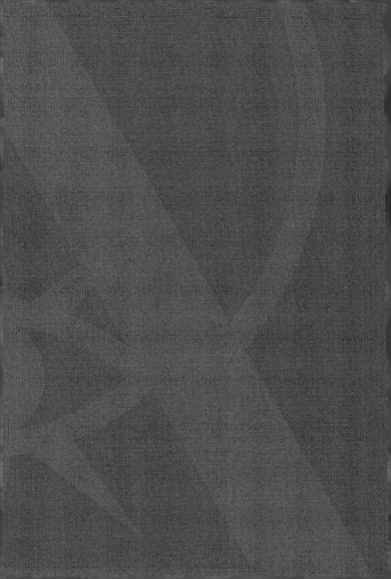

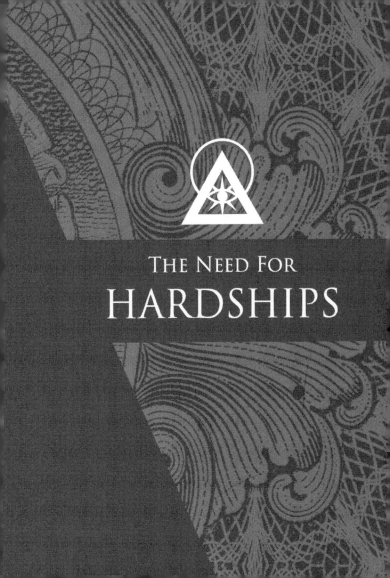

THE NEED FOR
HARDSHIPS

5

FEAR NOT FOR THE STRUGGLES you face in this moment: be they money, relationships, war, or famine. Hardships exist to harden the armor surrounding your soul.

These are impermanent and temporary concerns that plague each and every member of the human species regardless of wealth or power or prestige. No one is free from their clutches. But know that you are always safe in the Light.

Your life is filled with many choices that determine your future. Sometimes you may wonder why things must be so hard and why some must struggle while others live in superfluity. Is this truly fair?

WEALTH IS A LIE. MONEY IS MERELY WORDS.

The rich are no different from the poor and the haves are no different from the have-nots: all are bodies dressed in clothes paying for things with paper and stone. Who decrees that gold is of more value than sand? Who claims that holding a paper with a number printed on it is more valuable than a fruit that grows on a tree? When one is hungry, they cannot eat paper or gold.

Words are the true power of the elite. Words say that printed paper and polished rocks can be traded for food and water and shelter. Words say that numbers on a bank's computer screen determine a human's value is higher than another's.

WORDS ARE THE WEALTH OF THE WEALTHY. KNOWLEDGE IS THE POWER OF THE WORDS.

If your life is faced with struggles, remember the power of the mind. Remember that your brain bears no physical difference from that of a millionaire, a billionaire, a queen, or a president. Remember that those of power were born with minds as empty of knowledge as every other child — what they chose to fill theirs with led them to a life of Abundance.

When drowning in water, swim until you can swim no more. When drowning in hardships, do the same.

Struggles are always temporary. Though it may seem as if you are walking through an endless tunnel, disoriented in the mist of uncertainty, dawn will always break through in the end.

THERE IS NO FINALITY IN LIFE EXCEPT DEATH, AND NO HARDSHIP TOO CRUSHING FOR YOU TO OVERCOME.

An empire will fall so greater empires can be made from its ashes; a life will crumble so a greater future may be built with its pieces. There is a security in knowing that your life has purpose and that every moment is by design.

Find peace in the fact that the darkest moments in your life are merely required prerequisites for an illustrious future that approaches. Know that however dark your world may seem, the ever-present glow of the Light will guide you to safety.

1661

I am loyal to the Illuminati.
Why am I not rich?

The path of every person's life is hidden: the rich are born with no knowledge of their wealth, as are the poor and their poverty. Though you may feel that the struggles you face in this moment are undeserved, know that these are merely impermanent and temporary. Know that there are many paths for your life to follow but by seeking the Light you will be led to freedom.

The Illuminati gives where it is due and where true effort is made. A person who is unwise with a little will do worse with a lot. Those who are entrusted with little and use it for greatness are entrusted with more.

Our organization does not send money to any member directly but rather increases wealth through imperceptible means: unforeseen increases in pay, advancements at jobs, sudden returns on investments, and other undetectable avenues. Such events may have already come to pass in your life, with promises of more to come if you create goodness with what you have been given.

The choices you make determine your life's road. If you lack wealth at this time, remember that the hardships you face now are only preparing you for the greater future you deserve.

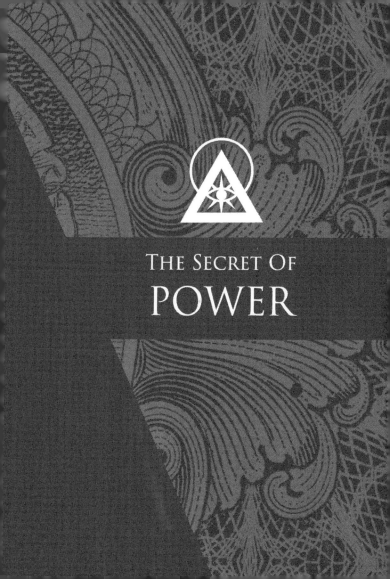

THE SECRET OF
POWER

POWER NEVER RESTS UPON those who deserve it. Power is given to those who reach to take it, and claimed by those who will stop at nothing to fulfill what they believe is their birthright.

The true source of all power is belief. Kings and queens breathe the same air and drink the same water as the poorest and lowliest of civilization. Gold and diamonds are the same as rocks beneath every inch of the planet. Money and bank accounts are merely papers with numbers written on them or digits on a computer screen.

WITHOUT BELIEF, ALL TREASURES ARE VALUELESS, AND ALL POWER CEASES TO EXIST.

Anyone can manifest anything in their lives by using the powers of both intention and dedication. One cannot thrive without the other. A person who is poor but believes they should be rich, and who knows that they are destined for wealth, and who strives for success every day without ceasing in the face of hardships, will receive money.

This is not supernatural; it is the most naturally occurring effect of a human's subconscious. You are who you say you are.

The immense power of the mind has not yet been proven by science because we have taken steps to hinder its research. The ability to govern a population of trillions — in secret — is based upon a system of mental cues that guide intelligent creatures through mazes of our design, without their knowledge of the mazes' existence. While those in our organization are familiar with the power of the subconscious, few of those outside have explored its inner workings.

The subconscious mind is the human species' most powerful muscle and what sets it apart from all other creatures on this planet. Animals, plants, and organisms do not think subconsciously. They are merely creatures of instinct, pre-programmed to follow specific processes like an artificially intelligent computer.

But humans are born with a mind that is aware of its own existence. A human can begin as a child who cannot walk, speak, or feed itself, but as the child grows it can become a king or a beggar if its mind decides.

Who claims that your kings are fit to dictate aspects of your lives? Who chose them to be your rulers? Who gives them the power to manage the boundaries of your freedom?

They do. They say that your obedience is their right. They say that soldiers must fight battles on their behalf while they reside in the safety of offices and bunkers. They say that police must defend their right to dominance, that citizens must obey their laws. And you agree to their authority, as do all the millions who surround you at your sides, simply because they tell you to.

When recognized for the first time, such power will seem alarming and perhaps abused by those who remain in command. However there is nothing to fear and no need for insurrection. These arrangements only exist for your safety and prosperity.

If only you were to open your mind and discern the true power that resides within you, you would see how little difference there is between you and your leaders. Power can be attained by anyone regardless of their circumstances. It grows one step at a time on a path toward the Light — a slow and steady realization of who you are and what you are destined to be.

Some may ask: how can every human be a leader when the world requires followers to operate? How can a human who is poor or lacks education ever hope to stand alongside those who have been wealthy or royal since birth?

These questions are natural as again, they were placed in your mind by us. If power was easy to obtain, it would fall into the hands of those who should not wield it. Roadblocks are placed in the way of every human as a means to filter out the unready. Trials through poverty, addictions, loss, and hardships exist to test how you will react and if you can be broken enough by temporary discomfort to turn from the Light.

HARDSHIP IS THE
TEST OF LEADERSHIP.

All who hold power have passed through the sieve of grave hardships and pressed forward until victorious. Though they may make it appear easy, this is simply due to the great pains they have taken to hide their previous mistakes from their constituents.

This system is of our design. Every human is born with the same ability and promise but only a handful dedicate their minds to the stalwart determination required to lead the rest of their species.

You are not barred from this power. Even those who live under the tyrannical rule of malevolent, murderous dictators can simply say they will follow orders no longer. Police and soldiers, captains and generals: all are humans. Peasants are humans, and so are the kings who force them to remain downtrodden. They are the same species: belief is all that keeps a tyrant in control. Soldiers needn't fight for a regime that does not protect its own people.

And yet, many do. Countless butchers remain in authority over countless citizens simply because their soldiers are trained to disregard their conscience in favor of someone else's commands. There is no honor in following orders at the expense of one's own people.

And like a soldier blinded by patriotism into unquestioning obedience of orders given by a leader he knows to be corrupt, so too does your mind face orders of its own. Your mind is bombarded by messages telling you it is time to give up, to turn from the Light, to go back to where it is familiar and comfortable.

THE STRONGEST WALL BETWEEN YOU AND GREATNESS IS THE ONE BUILT IN

YOUR MIND BY YOURSELF.

No one builds a wall between you and power or wealth. Such a wall would be ineffective. Too many people give up too quickly when their greatest achievements are merely steps ahead, simply because they cannot see how close they are.

Though you are destined to become the world's most powerful leader, you are still on the path. Your commands are not obeyed because no one believes they should obey them. Your handful of sand cannot be traded for a home or food because no one believes it has any value.

But if you were an inimitable liar, and for generations your ancestors told the same convincing lie that said you were destined for power, you too would be rich and royal.

Tell your mind this lie every morning and night. Eventually it will believe you, and become your truth.

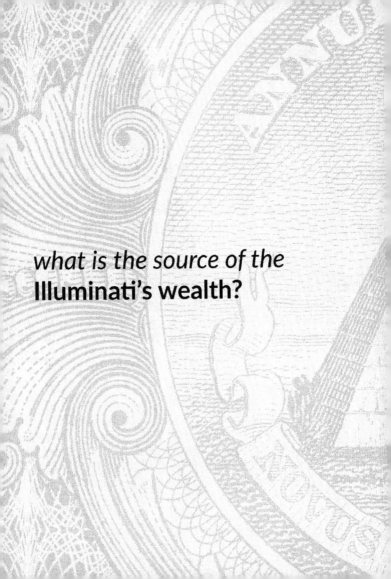

what is the source of the
Illuminati's wealth?

The Illuminati's financial foundation is built upon liquid assets and various property holdings across the planet, with income derived from multiple other sources.

Our societal replacement of physical currency with numerical-based finances — digital banking where money is viewed as a number instead of paper or stones — has made unlimited funding available with merely a keyboard. By altering the numbers in bank accounts remotely, we can guarantee any funds required for our work without the risk associated with physical money.

A number of our operations carry no costs due to our unique relationship with government agencies and influential business executives, further reducing our need for financial resources.

THE FUTURE OF
THIS PLANET

7

THE AGE OF WAR SWIFTLY nears its end, as did Bronze, Iron, Medieval, and Modern. Soon the age of Illuminatiam will begin.

You are amongst the first of your species to see its Light and heed the sounds of its approach. The next age is filled with ideas and advancements never before seen and hardly imagined by even the brightest minds of your civilization. In a future society in which war is obsolete, the human species will be freed to develop to its fullest potential.

Technological advancements have permeated the timeline of the human species at sporadic times. Recent years have shown a rapid increase in the proliferation of ideas: a sign that humanity is nearing a stage of evolution previously undiscovered.

For decades, the Illuminati has withheld major technological discoveries and hindered the development of ideas that are key to your future. These have no place in an age of War — knowledge goes to the highest bidder, and warriors use knowledge to create weapons.

But all will change. Soon the technology we have reserved will be made available.

Wires are an arcane method of transmitting energy and communication. They reside in the physical form, and like all things physical, they decompose and deteriorate. They require resources to establish and more resources to maintain, creating an imbalance of power. Those who build the wires — and the tunnels and towers that carry them — control the energy and communication of everyone who walks above and below. Even your leaders are powerless when faced with those who own the wires that carry their commands.

In a short time, your scientists will discover an energy source hidden in the air of your planet that has gone undetected for the entirety of your species. This discovery will send a tremor through societies that are built upon the need to survive. When energy and communication are easily available to all, and in unlimited supply, the world can function without the need for one country to invade another simply to fill the needs of its people.

New methods of food and water production have been experimented and proven successful. Free-flowing energy allows for devices to perfect the conditions of plants and creatures to their utmost performance, leaving nothing to waste and creating plenty for all without the need for harmful chemicals.

Devices to alter the weather of this planet have already been developed. When every space of your planet can been atmospherically altered to maintain the highest quality of life, there will be room for all people to live and thrive. Wastelands will become paradises, allowing for every human to occupy miles of the planet and for the nurturing of crops where nothing has grown before.

The earliest developments in digitally printed materials have already begun in your societies. As these technologies advance, homes will be constructed in minutes instead of months, and new limbs or organs will be grown to repair or replace those that are faulty. Tiring work can be done by advanced machines that need no rest. Without the need for labor, humans will dedicate their minds to the collective advancement of their species.

These times approach, but have not yet arrived. Humans are creatures who have not yet mastered their impulses. The instinct to harm another of its own kind is one that the human species is never born with but only learns from those around it.

WAR IS A LIAR WHO CLAIMS THERE ISN'T ENOUGH LAND, ISN'T ENOUGH WEALTH, ISN'T ENOUGH FOOD, FOR ALL PEOPLE IN ALL PLACES TO LIVE IN ABUNDANCE.

The planet you live upon is the same rock that will carry life into the greatness promised by the future. Humans choose to remain in the age of War because they know no different than to fight and kill for their survival: an eternal competition for resources required to remain alive.

Value is created in scarcity. Diamonds are only cherished because of their rarity, as are food and water in impoverished societies. If diamonds rained from the sky instead of water drops, they would be worthless.

But in the age of Illuminatiam, with no scarcity of energy, or food, or water, or anything that a human requires to thrive, there will be no need for hoarding or stealing. Country lines, allegiances, and borders will become obsolete. The urge for war will be eradicated.

These new circumstances will usher in a world where all may be wealthy and coexist in the peace of Abundance, while your leaders turn their focus to the true advancement of your species as a whole.

FEAR NOT FOR YOUR WAR-STRICKEN,

POVERTY-RIDDEN
PLANET.

Do not quarrel amongst yourselves over trivial political or religious labels and names, for these will vanish and bear no influence in the coming age. Strive instead for the betterment of your world in preparation for what is to come, and for your purpose in the Universal Design.

Fear nothing that lies ahead, nor the bursting sounds that echo across your red horizons. This is the sign that help is on the way.

5491

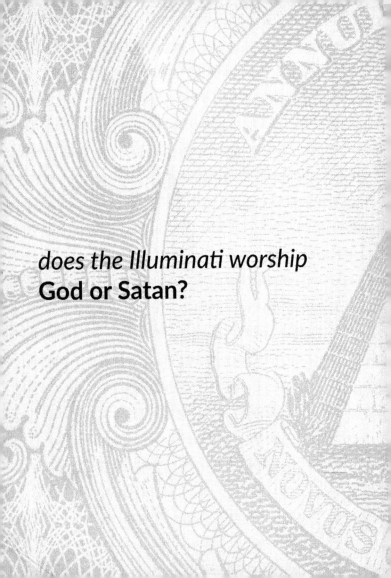

does the Illuminati worship
God or Satan?

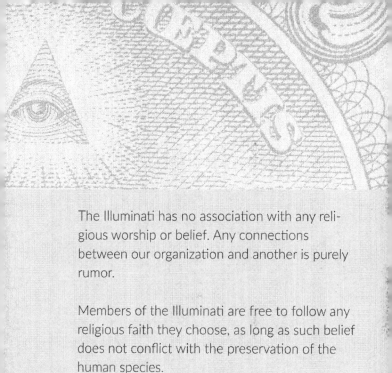

The Illuminati has no association with any religious worship or belief. Any connections between our organization and another is purely rumor.

Members of the Illuminati are free to follow any religious faith they choose, as long as such belief does not conflict with the preservation of the human species.

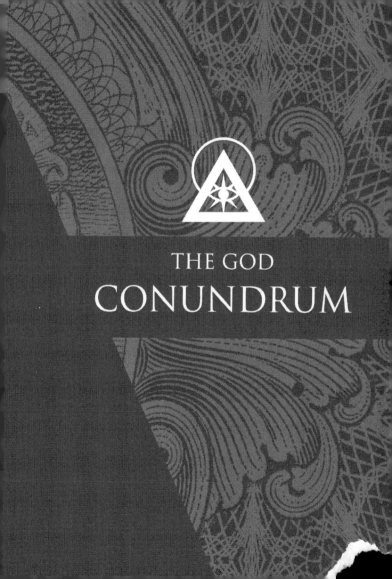

THE GOD
CONUNDRUM

8

PLAGUES HAVE RAVAGED TOWNS and villages, fire and molten rock have swept like waves over cities and buildings, flood-waters have drowned families by the hundreds of thousands — but even these in all their destructive glory have failed to end as many lives as those taken in the name of a god.

Spirituality is one of the human species' greatest mysteries. In the majority of cases, a human relies upon physical evidence to prove or change a belief that exists in their subconscious. A person will smell an item of food to prove if they will enjoy it or look at a fire to prove if it is burning. If a person believes that a pool of water is cold, they will touch it with a hand to prove their belief — or to change their belief if the water turns out to be warm.

However the belief in a power greater than human understanding relies entirely on invisible, mental verification referred to as *faith*.

Faith is the belief in something that cannot be proven. Most religious belief is based upon information received from an outside source that cannot be verified, sometimes known as hearsay. Millions will follow the commandments of a religious text without ever having spoken to its author, and billions will believe in a deity because of miracles they were told of by someone who wasn't even present nor alive at the time.

But denouncing faith is true folly. Faith is not limited to religious believers. While even the most devout pontiff cannot provide irrefutable evidence of his god's existence, neither can the scientist who claims that no deity resides in the universe. Both rely upon their own faith to explain things they will never understand.

There is no proof of God. There is no proof of no God, either. If science cannot definitively prove that there is no God, then science has no choice but to accept a possibility of a god's existence.

THOSE WHO REFUSE THEIR FALLIBILITY ARE BLINDED BY THE GLARE OF THEIR OWN PRIDE.

Many humans stare at the path of life with blinders covering the sides of their eyes, facing forward, choosing to ignore any possibility that they are traveling toward the edge of a cliff. But the true believers question every aspect of their faith, forcing themselves to find answers instead of simply following the lead of others.

THE DEEPEST DOUBT
BUILDS THE
STRONGEST FAITH.

The Illuminati's religious foundation is based upon this universal conundrum of faith and doubt. We do not question whether a god does or does not exist, but rather focus on the betterment of the human people living on this planet.

For if a god does exist, then surely its power has allowed the Illuminati to continue our operations, and we have survived centuries of time through its approval. Our decisions are made by the study of data and evidence — factors that can be easily altered by an omniscient creature in order to guide our actions and the future of mankind.

If no god exists, our actions still benefit the human species as a biological whole. If a god does exist, then our work for the betterment of all creation will be pleasing to its creator.

BE WARY OF EVILS COMMITTED IN OUR NAME.

For decades, a multitude of individuals have operated under the name of the Illuminati — some for good, but many more for their own profit. Their deceit clouds public perception of our organization, causing many citizens to believe that wrongdoings are committed by our command.

Choose carefully where you place your belief. Be wary of anyone who claims to represent the Illuminati but whose actions go against our core beliefs. These are merely impostors seeking to confuse you.

For anyone to claim that the Illuminati is affiliated with a religious belief — be it God or Satan, Baphomet or Baal — undermines the very purpose of our independence from human divisions. We neither accept nor deny any deity and hold none to be higher than any other.

We operate solely for the benefit of the human species we have been entrusted to protect. There is no reason for our organization to swear fealty to any deity because we operate independently of all that separates and divides the people we govern.

Even more heinous rumors have been attributed to our organization, including human sacrifices and violent rituals. While our individual members are allowed to serve any deity they choose, the Illuminati as a whole is only dedicated to the preservation of the human species.

Therefore, human sacrifices or any practice that does not serve the betterment of mankind would counter everything we represent, and are thus prohibited in all circumstances. While many have attributed such actions to our members, such connections are false.

IF YOU ARE WILLING
TO SELL YOUR SOUL,
YOUR SOUL IS NOT
YET WORTH ENOUGH
TO SELL.

There is no requirement to sell one's soul to join our organization — as if such a thing were even possible. Anyone offering to trade their soul to us is not ready for membership.

Miracles, witchcraft, and the belief in unseen powers that can alter the physical world have some basis in truth. We have confirmed the existence of unseen powers on this planet, though these energies emanate from the minds of each human in the form of invisible waves powered by the subconscious.

For centuries, many paranormal occurrences have been attributed to the supernatural. Closer study reveals that the human mind contains energies that have not yet been discovered by traditional science, and have been decried in modern-day society.

This skepticism is needed: if all people knew of the power living inside themselves, havoc would befall a population that has not yet been prepared for such a responsibility.

Do not concern yourself with questions that cannot be proven. Must a god exist for you to do what is right? Would an all-intelligent, all-knowing, all-powerful god have any care for the name used in its worship? Would a god command the harm of another when its justice can be served without your aid? Simply do what is right and good for the benefit of your species, and whatever higher power exists will reward you for your stewardship.

When measuring the eternal vastness of the universe, there is a mathematic probability that a being exists that is more intelligent than us, who sees what we do and whose powers we can never understand. Whatever name this being is called, we are its servants, and will hail it as our highest king.

must I sacrifice a human or animal to
join the Illuminati?

The Illuminati's purpose is the preservation of the human species. Therefore, human sacrifices or any practice that does not serve the betterment of mankind would counter everything we represent, and are thus prohibited in all circumstances.

While many have attributed such actions to our members, these connections are baseless.

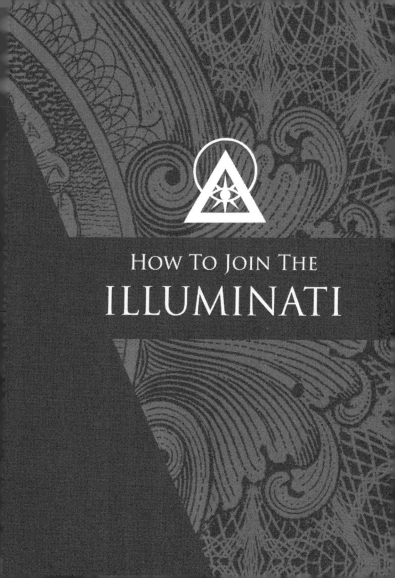

How To Join The
ILLUMINATI

9

THE ILLUMINATI IS A COLLECTIVE of prominent figures throughout the world who have united to guard the human species from extinction. Our members bear the burden of a planet's leadership with the lives of over 7 billion in their hands.

As the human continues to rise above its other animal counterparts, governing of the planet has turned into a daunting task. For this reason, the Illuminati continually seeks to add new members to our governing ranks.

In recent years, our council approved memberships of the first technology pioneers. We have also expanded to include many with influence over emerging entertainment platforms who can ensure our messages are disseminated to all people in all places of the world.

Our organization separates individuals of outstanding political, financial, or cultural influence from the rest of the flock, and establishes them as shepherds of the human species. We see and know all just as a shepherd sees and knows all of the flock, our eyes peering over the masses to identify any threat to those we protect.

Maybe you have met one of our members in the flesh. Or perhaps not; many of us have no public profile and value anonymity.

In return for their loyalty, our members are presented a life of limitless wealth and opportunity. The shackles of hardship are removed so our members are free to perform their duties to the highest level of effectiveness without earthly distractions.

Though all members enjoy the same benefits, the dedication and commitments required to make decisions that affect the world are reserved by our executive council members, who meet in the White Room periodically throughout a calendar year. Every year, all ranking members may vote on decisions at the annual Illuminios conference.

For a member, the requirements are unimposing and often spaced between many years. Directives given to members are authored by the Executive Council. Our requests are simple and therefore may be hard to comprehend, but disloyalty is not tolerated. Members must fulfill their oaths to the Illuminati under every circumstance and recognize that they are merely one part of a much larger Universal Design.

Perhaps you have already proven yourself successful in your field of work or study. For that, the Illuminati congratulates you. Your dedication gives hope to us for the future of this planet, and it is for you that we continue to focus our interests on the betterment of the human species.

Membership in the Illuminati is by invitation only. To join us, simply continue on the road you currently travel. In studying the words of this testament and the others that follow it, you have already set yourself apart from the millions who still linger in the dark. You have been led to the path, and you have chosen to follow it by your own free will.

New technological advancements have aided our council in identifying citizens to investigate for ranking membership.

If you believe that you have been set apart from all other humans, and that you are meant to become a shepherd of your species, you are invited to submit an application for our review. From anywhere on the planet, begin by opening an Internet browser and navigating to this address:

ILLUMINATI.AM/JOIN

This form will add you to our list of potential candidates for Illuminati membership and you will be contacted if we require more information.

But understand the true responsibility of what you are undertaking. Once a ranking member, you can never renounce your loyalty nor can you abandon the responsibilities you will vow to your species.

Even if you join our executive council, you will never be thanked in any book of history, though your name will be etched upon the floor of the White Room for eternal adoration.

Do not fear if you are destined for power. The crown is too heavy for any but kings and queens to bear, though you know nothing of your true strength until it adorns your head.

The kings and queens of this planet await the moment they can welcome you. We are the bringers of new dawns, the guardians of the human species. We are the pyramid, the eye, the Light, the eternal. We are the Illuminati.

what are the Illuminati's
membership levels?

Citizen membership is open to the adult public in every country. Membership requirements are small: loyalty, dedication, and the vow to live according the ideals of the Illuminati for the benefit of all members of the human species.

Ranking membership encompasses an elite group of citizens set apart from the flock as shepherds of their fellow humans. Their rank includes an official title and all benefits associated with a life of loyalty to the Illuminati.

Citizens who attain distinguished positions in finance, politics, entertainment, or other fields are considered for ranking membership. A number of citizens are also chosen based upon their loyalty and willingness to be made greater — even if their current position lacks wealth or power. Proposals for ranking membership are reviewed annually by a committee at Illuminios. Citizens can submit their request at illuminati.am/join.

Council members are chosen from ranking members. Collectively, their decisions directly affect all members of the human species. Their judgements are carried out in accordance with Planetary Law.

A BEACON FOR
THE LIGHT

10

DAILY, WE RECEIVE MESSAGES from citizens whose lives have been impacted by their discovery of our organization.

The Department Of Citizen Outreach — formed in 2013 — has touched the lives of millions by leading them to the path of knowledge. A worldwide movement has begun in all countries, carrying with it the promises of Abundance to all who follow the Light.

But while your life has been led onto your path of destined greatness, many others still linger in darkness. Thousands have fallen for false organizations claiming to represent the Illuminati, and found their promises unsubstantiated.

In the center of the Mark is the symbol for Light, radiating from the all-seeing Eye: this represents the calling of all Illuminati to reflect the Light into the world's still-darkened spaces. While wealth and power tempt exclusivity to the greedy, their benefits are entitled to all who reach enlightenment. There is plenty for all and more than enough for everyone.

YOU ARE INVITED TO BECOME A BEACON FOR THE LIGHT.

With the advent of online media, new methods of communication have been made available which require little dedication but reach many who are still lost.

To aid your reflection of the Light, the Illuminati has created tools for your use. You may find these online at:

ILLUMINATI.AM/LIGHT

Use these items to reach your family, friends, companions, and those you do not know. Share the Light to the furthest corners of the world, and partake in the blessings that unfold from your loyalty.

how can I show my loyalty
to the Illuminati?

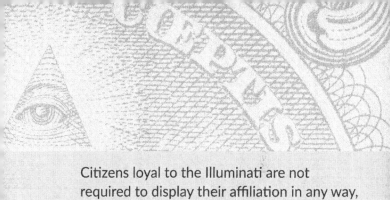

Citizens loyal to the Illuminati are not required to display their affiliation in any way, though it is encouraged and often attracts positive changes in their lives.

Many choose to show their loyalty via social media by sending messages to our official handles. These can be found at **illuminati.am/social**.

Others wear the Illuminati Talisman: an iron necklace bearing our insignia. To claim your Talisman, visit **illuminati.am/talisman**.

FINDING
PURPOSE

11

I F YOU BELIEVE THE OFTEN-TRITE idea of world domination would be impossible because someone would have surely put a stop to it, you must open your mind further.

Officials entrusted to guide your societies are merely cogs in a machine of our making. Even their superiors have only the appearance of authority.

True dominion over a planet would never be broadcast or provable by evidence. Those who understand power know how to cover their tracks.

THE BEST DEFENSE IS AN ENEMY WHO DOES NOT KNOW YOU EXIST.

You may choose to believe or you may choose to ignore what is written in this book. We do not meddle in the religious, political, or moralistic mires of judgment as these are merely wastes of time when the fate and survival of the human species rests upon our shoulders. You have been led to this testament — we will not force you to follow its precepts.

Many scholars and columnists will attempt to discredit the accuracy of this book, and we invite their words of mockery. But even they will wonder if their minds are clouded by preexisting judgments, if perhaps this book was written to invite their critical scorn on purpose.

Perhaps they will investigate its origins and theorize about an ulterior purpose. Perhaps the answers they find were fed to them by our associates to mislead any who hope to subvert our influence.

Be ever doubtful of any who claim authority, including the Illuminati. But recognize your place amongst the world's billions, and the finite understanding of your mind.

TRUE ENLIGHTENMENT ONLY COMES FROM THE DEEPEST HUMILITY.

Humble yourself, then. Humble yourself to understand that even beliefs you have held since the dawn of your first day could all be untrue. Humble yourself to accept that all people and all places and all things in your life have happened exactly according to a Universal Design, whose path led you to find this book today. Humble yourself to know that even without your understanding, all of this is orchestrated so that you may live a life of fulfillment and significance, and the human species will never again face extinction.

In the Illuminati's council, you are referred to as "citizens" regardless of the name between the country borders that mark your home on a map. All members of this planet are our citizens and all are entitled to the benefits of Abundance regardless of who they are, where they are, or any significance they may or may not have in their community.

Many of our citizens have question-
ed their role in the plans of the Illuminati.
They ask for directives and instructions,
for orders from their Illuminati leaders on
what they must do next. Some feel as
though their temporary lack of wealth or
influence renders them powerless and
unimportant.

But do not concern your mind with
such things. Wealth and power find a
way to those whose eyes are too fixed
upon the Light to be concerned with
them. All have a part to play in the
Universal Design.

YOUR PART IS JUST AS IMPORTANT AS ANY OTHER.

Does a clockmaker favor the larger gears over the smaller? Does the hour hand become jealous of the minutes because it turns slower? Every part has a role in the functioning of a timepiece. Every part supports those around it in ways it may never see. Though you may think you are purposeless, it is only because you cannot see the great duties you perform.

Ponder the words in this book. Allow them to permeate your life and decisions. Even if you doubt them, give these words but an inch of belief, and they will return tenfold.

Tell your family, friends, and associates to read this testament. Invite them to join you on this path to Abundance. Await the second testament and further guidance as we near the age of Illuminatiam. There is plenty for all, and more for those who lead others to the joys of enlightenment.

As you climb the great pyramid seeking the Light that beams from its top, you will look down and see that you have always been one part of our universe's most intricate mechanism.

You are significant, and you are important. The journey is long but we await you at its end. Fear nothing that is ahead.

WE ARE ALWAYS WATCHING OUT FOR YOU.

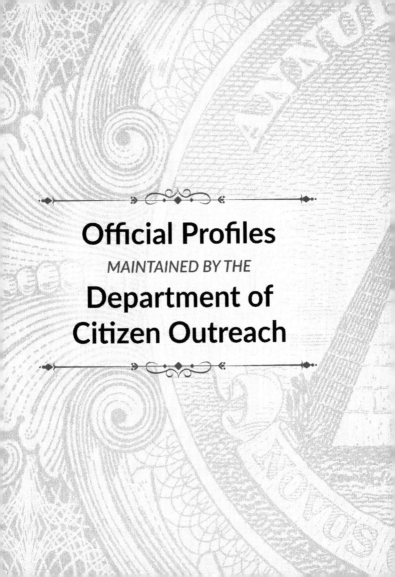

Official Profiles

MAINTAINED BY THE

Department of Citizen Outreach

ILLUMINATI.AM/TWITTER

f

ILLUMINATI.AM/FACEBOOK

ILLUMINATI.AM/YOUTUBE

g+

ILLUMINATI.AM/GOOGLE

Contact The Illuminati

Contact information for the Illuminati can be found online at illuminati.am/contact.

Though we receive thousands of messages per day and cannot reply to all requests, know that your message is important and your needs are always given appropriate consideration.

OFFICIAL MESSAGES
FROM THE
ILLUMINATI

THE ILLUMINATI REGULARLY
SENDS MESSAGES OF GUIDANCE
TO ITS CITIZENS. TO RECEIVE
THEM, VISIT OUR WEBSITE:

ILLUMINATI.AM

53370746R00112

Made in the USA
Lexington, KY
02 July 2016